Self-discipline
The key to achieving your goals.

Ella G. peterson

Table of contents

Introduction (what you need to know about self-discipline)

Self-discipline is the capacity to go on, maintain motivation, and act despite any physical or mental discomfort. You demonstrate it when you consciously decide to strive toward improving yourself, even in the face of obstacles like diversions, difficulty, or bad circumstances.

Self-discipline is distinct from willpower or self-motivation. Persistence, the capacity to carry out your ideas, and hard effort are all factors that go into it, as well as motivation and willpower.

Why Exercise Self-Discipline?

Self-discipline is beneficial in many aspects of our life.
For example, it motivates you to do excellent work even when you don't feel like

it. Even when you're ready to give up, it provides you the courage to maintain your professionalism with your clientele. It aids in your perseverance and achievement of the goals you set for yourself. You may achieve tremendous success through self-discipline even when the odds seem overwhelming to others.

Additionally, it may promote performance and learning. According to studies, pupils who exhibit a high level of self-discipline retain more information than those who do not. Additionally, studies found that disciplined pupils do better because they are more meticulous in their work. [1]

A person's degree of self-discipline is a better predictor of success than their IQ, according to research, which also supports this claim.

Similar to a muscle, self-discipline becomes stronger the more you use it and try to build it. But it's crucial to avoid setting too

ambitious first objectives. Instead, establish modest objectives and gradually raise the amount of difficulty over time. You'll become better the more you practice.
It's important to develop self-discipline in life. Self-discipline is what enables us to do high-quality work. It keeps us pursuing our goals through tough times. And it helps us to stay professional, even when we're not feeling great.

Chapter 1

The four cornerstones of self-discipline

Cornerstone#1:RELAXED DISCIPLINE

We've somehow developed the belief that to become better, we must fight our own battles. Self-discipline is unquestionably a component of greater knowledge, but it isn't, can't be, and shouldn't come from the ego-driven, restless intellect.

We must first learn to relax, that correct before we can develop calm self-discipline. Although it seems so simple, cultivating the proper level of relaxation takes practice. Because we've been taught since we were little that self-discipline requires restraint, punishment, and, yes, even physical tension.

WHAT SEEMS LIKE A RELAXED FORM OF DISCIPLINE?

It has a feeling of dynamic balance within. You don't berate yourself for mistakes you make. Bring your concentration to the work gradually and, while being calm, give it your whole attention. Forget to complete a task? No issue! Breathe out, relax your shoulders, and consider your next move.

Everyone's everyday duties are carried out with a perceptible feeling of comfort and "flow," as seen from the outside. People can tell you're calm on the outside, which adds to their feeling of serenity. You're giving the world something tremendously valuable.

What does relaxed discipline not look like?

In the first place, relaxed discipline is not an excuse. Additionally, it's not something you do sometimes. It's a way of living, an ethos. Like any worthwhile activity, it calls for dedication and perseverance.

CORNERSTONE #3: FAMILIARIZATION AND HABITUATION

Automaticity will continue to direct most of what you do unless you're some type of enlightened entity. Thus, developing, establishing, and adopting healthy behaviors is crucial.

Why not just state, "Build new habits"? Considering that it is too sudden, unclear, and, certainly, terrifying. After all, developing habits may be challenging. A new habit doesn't merely "come" to one. Because of our misguided attitude to self-discipline, the development process is often wrought with unneeded stress, strain, and self-doubt.

So, in keeping with our laid-back, methodical approach, we're going to talk about habits in a slightly different way.

FAMILIARIZATION

Implementing the habit and repeatedly reinforcing it as healthy are both parts of familiarization. This implies that we continue to be alert to and sensitive to the development that results from the establishment of new habits. then, when the habit has been established, remember the advantages. This needs some background since familiarization might be misleading. Let's spend a moment discussing weight reduction.

To feel better about themselves, people lose weight. They decide to act because they are fed up with their weight.

Many individuals struggle. According to one estimate, up to 98% of people left. Ninety percent of those who do lose weight do so within two years, on average. Both result from failing to pay attention to the procedure.
People often make poor decisions, which trigger still more poor decisions. They lose

touch with the experience of losing weight, its advantages, or the negative effects of doing so or failing to do so. As a consequence, the need to continue the habit fades, a process psychologists refer to as normalization. We just become "accustomed to" having certain things, acting a particular way, etc. It ceases to be a major issue. (Normalization is, incidentally, a significant factor in the proverb "money can't buy happiness.

Even the things we've worked so hard to obtain begin to slip our minds. We run the danger of losing those goods when this occurs.

As a result, we must "Renew thyself entirely each day; do it again, and again, and eternally again," as Henry David Thoreau says in "Walden." The practice of thankfulness is one method for achieving this.

Don't overlook the action's cause, effects, and advantages.

CORNERSTONE #3: ATTENTION AND CONCENTRATION

It's not an exaggeration to say that your capacity for focus is your most precious possession. Most undertakings, including all forms of training, depending on your capacity to concentrate and maintain it. Of course, this includes all attempts at self-discipline

But first, we have to accept the unpleasant truth: most of us have terrible attention spans.

There are several causes behind this, but convenience may be the main offender. We are used to receiving stuff promptly. Within a day, we may purchase a product from across the nation and have it delivered to our home. Impatience is the antithesis of calm, stable attention.

CORNERSTONE #4: COMPASSION AND FORGIVENESS

A strong mind is sympathetic. A caring mind is a powerful tool for the development of oneself. How?

First, having compassion for oneself will enable you to see any perceived flaws or "failures" in a completely new light. Perhaps the single biggest obstacle to self-discipline is being too tough on oneself.

Because it increases resilience, compassion is effective and relevant. You're going to make mistakes sometimes; everyone does. It will all depend on your capacity to get back up again and to do it with a caring, loving, and forgiving heart.

It may have been a few days or perhaps a few years since you last tried to improve yourself. Maybe you're not up to the work or feel useless.

I'm here to let you know that all of this is mental rubbish. Don't allow your reasons to get in the way of what you want to do.

So, this is your conclusion. If you want to become a better version of yourself, practice a relaxed discipline, develop your attention, cultivate self-compassion, forgive yourself for your faults, and create long-lasting, process-oriented habits.

Love yourself and others around you first and foremost. The most significant kind of self-improvement is that.

Chapter 2

Types of self-discipline

There are various methods by which we may employ self-discipline habits daily. Here are instances of three types: active discipline, reactive discipline, and proactive discipline.

Active discipline means doing what you need to at that particular time such as eating a good meal, minimizing your distractions while studying, and exercising.
You were actively disciplined when you opted to eat healthy instead of unhealthy. You were disciplined when you made the time to study and put your phone off. Another example came when you choose to

work out instead than watch TV or browsing the internet.

Reactive discipline involves managing your thoughts or actions while dealing with unanticipated scenarios such as receiving a flat tire on your way to work, dealing with an unpleasant individual, and locking your vehicle keys in your car.
Instead of grumbling, you utilized these challenges as chances to grow. When you received the flat tire, you had the tire repaired. At that time, you decided to be glad because it was simply a flat tire and no one was wounded.
When dealing with the disrespectful individual, you turned the other cheek. You recognized that their rudeness was their problem and not yours. You realized that "an eye for an eye" renders everyone blind. You opted to treat that individual with additional compassion since they needed it.
You locked your vehicle keys in the car. You thought to yourself, "It's alright, errors

happen." You know the necessity of forgiving yourself and moving forward. You realize that this is simply one tiny obstacle throughout your complete 24-hour day.

Proactive discipline involves doing things in advance in an attempt to better manage a circumstance such as carrying an umbrella on a wet day, establishing a to-do list, and getting to bed on time.
You watched the news that morning and prepared for the weather. You had goals that you needed to fulfill on a deadline and chose to make a to-do list to prioritize those tasks. Instead of staying up late, you opted to go to bed early to get up on time the following day.

Admittedly, it is hard to commit to self-discipline daily. Self-discipline is no simple achievement since we are continuously presented with challenges that appear to emerge at the most troublesome moment.

We indeed have no control over what might happen but we do have power over how we respond to what occurs. We also have access and a chance to practice skills that help us to exercise self-discipline and accomplish our goals.

Chapter 3

importance of self-discipline

Self-discipline enables you to remain focused on your objectives. It permits you to remain in control of yourself and of your attitude to any event. Self-discipline is like a muscle: the more you exercise it, the stronger you get. Lack of self-discipline may generate poor self-esteem.

1. Self-Discipline Helps You Resist Temptations

There always have been, and there will always be temptations.

Temptations are aimed to pull you away from what it is that is proper, or what it is that you are supposed to be doing.

When your mind is permitted to roam, you allow yourself to picture where you may end up if you were to give in to your desires.

There is generally a negative meaning linked with temptations, which may usually end in you finding yourself in some difficulties.

However, being self-disciplined permits you to reject the temptations that you find your mind questioning. Recognizing that you have big-picture objectives, you are more likely to have the willpower to say 'No' to what may look like the more tempting alternative in the short term.

2. Self-Discipline Increases Your Focus

When you are self-disciplined, you can stay focused on the work at hand. There will always be diversions and temptations around you.

However, when you are self-disciplined, you appreciate the value of the task you are working on. You also know that the hard effort you are putting in will play a greater part in what you are aiming to accomplish.

Remaining focused is half the fight. When you have a clear grasp of your objectives and strategy to reach them, you have the self-discipline to remain focused and keep chasing your aspirations. When others are making excuses or seeking reasons to leave, you continue to stay focused and work relentlessly.

3. Self-Disciplines Helps You To Remain Motivated When You Aren't Seeing Results
It is challenging to stay motivated when you don't see any benefits from your hard work, or when you are locked in a routine that doesn't encourage pleasure or satisfaction. There will always be such days, regardless of where you are at in your life.

However, you will find it simpler to stay motivated when you can be more disciplined in how you choose to spend your time. When you are disciplined with your time, it helps to keep you involved in the activity you are taking part in.

Too much of anything is a negative thing and may lead to you becoming uninspired with your approach to many elements of your life. As described in greater depth in the following part, you should attempt to live a balanced life as it helps to enhance your motivation.

4. Self-Discipline Helps To Promote A Balanced Lifestyle

Self-discipline is having the capacity to be doing what you are required to be doing, it doesn't necessarily imply you should be hard at work.

Like everything in life, balance is crucial, and being self-disciplined helps to foster a balanced existence.

Without having time set out to relax, laugh, have fun, to spend time with family and friends, you will rapidly begin to burn out. Productivity will diminish, your drive won't be as high as it previously was and your view can begin to be less hopeful.

While having fun and taking breaks is vital, when you are self-disciplined, you can hold yourself responsible for how you go about doing those things.
An example may involve scheduling a break from work yet coming back to the job that needs completion when the break time is done. Or maybe you are diligent about the time you go to bed each night, so you put yourself in the best possible position to have a productive day tomorrow.

Life is about balance, your capacity to be self-disciplined helps to develop a life with balance.

5. Self-Discipline Improves The Relationships With Those In Your Life
Self-discipline will also help you to have better interactions with the many individuals in your life. You know the

significance of a friendship or a family member and have the discipline to keep these ties growing.

Instead of canceling arrangements last minute, you appreciate the significance of the connections you have and make the time for them. Furthermore, you are more present and engaged when you are around friends and family.
You have the self-discipline to listen and be helpful, instead of getting distracted by your surroundings or continuously checking your smartphone.
Others will notice the discipline you have in regards to your connection with them and attempt to reciprocate.

6. Self-Discipline Enables You To Be Healthier
Having the will strength to be self-disciplined may also assist with other parts of your life such as health and fitness.

Maybe more so than other aspects of your life, keeping healthy needs you to take action. You need to make regular good selections to generate the greatest outcomes.

Self-discipline concerning health and fitness is obvious in numerous different ways. It may include:

having the capacity to keep to a balanced diet to minimize meals heavy in fat or sugar

drinking more water since it helps keep you hydrated and boosts the efficacy of various body systems

being disciplined to exercise frequently encourages an active lifestyle and boosts the health of your heart and lungs

7. Self-Discipline Allows You To Achieve Your Goals More Quickly

Being self-disciplined is vital because it helps you attain your objectives more rapidly. You can get more done each day since you are rigorous about your timetables.

Distractions have a minor influence on your life since you are focused on your objectives and what you are attempting to attain. A lack of distractions implies more time for the things and people that are important to you such as fitness, friendships, hobbies, or spiritual convictions.

As a consequence, you live a more balanced lifestyle which boosts your productivity when it comes time to put in the effort that will assist you to attain your objectives.

Finally, being self-disciplined helps to increase your general attention towards what it is that you are working on. When you are concentrated, you can efficiently and successfully execute things. This helps you to achieve more in a shorter length of time.

8. Self-Discipline Helps You To Be The Best Version Of Yourself

Various aspects might help you become the greatest version of yourself, but

self-discipline is undoubtedly among the crucial ones.
When you can be disciplined with your activities, you can hold yourself responsible to live the life that you want to.

It supports a balanced lifestyle that pushes you to pursue your objectives with discipline, make time for those who are essential, and keep well so you are physically able to strive after your aspirations.

The awareness that there are 86,400 seconds each day. What are you doing now, so that tomorrow you are a step closer to where you want to be? If not now, then when?

Chapter 4

Discovering your motivation

Lack of motivation besets even the most successful individuals. If you've ever had a hard time living up to a New Year's resolution or completing any sort of goal, you're not alone. If you maintain your focus on the big picture, you may restore motivation and attain the final objectives you set for yourself. Learn more about how to find inspiration.

What Is Motivation?

Motivation is the internal driving force individuals rely upon to work hard and accomplish their objectives. Without this component of human nature, it would be hard to gain new talents, develop ourselves, and seek out new experiences. In general, motivation boils down to two broader categories: extrinsic and intrinsic motivation.

Extrinsic motivation refers to the urge to accomplish impacted by external causes. These external forces might either reward or punish you should you accomplish or not attain your objectives appropriately. Intrinsic motivation, by contrast, originates from the inside. While external influences may be able to keep you going periodically, the internal drive helps you maintain the road even when conditions appear grim.

How to Find Motivation

Learning how to find motivation requires practice and dedication. Keep these things in mind while you strive to spark your self-motivation:

1. Exercise when feasible. The endorphin rush you experience from exercise might

help raise your motivation levels, particularly when you work out outside and get some vitamin D in the sun. Additionally, each time you exercise, you show yourself you can set goals—however small—and accomplish them.

2. Fake it until you make it. To accomplish long-term objectives, continue through even on the days you feel uninspired and disengaged. Encountering this type of internal opposition is natural. The more times you work through it, the simpler it will be to unlock a flow state and restore the drive.

3. Practice self-care. As you discover how to become inspired, remember it's good to take pauses and to feel frustrated at times. Forgive yourself—self-compassion is one of the fundamental elements of self-motivation. You'll be back on track in no time. Give yourself tiny prizes for all your hard work, too. This form of self-care roots your feeling of success in a more concrete manner.

4. Seek inspiration. Try to locate resources you may rely on to keep yourself inspired and motivated to attain your objectives. Create an uplifting playlist of your favorite tunes. Listen to podcasts on the same things you desire to attain. Read self-improvement books to obtain a better understanding of how you may make your aspirations become reality. Try out applications that may help you plan out how to attain your objectives while also delivering you nuggets of inspiration along the road.

5. Set reasonable objectives. Do your best to create objectives you believe you can reach. When you create realistic goals for yourself, it takes less time to attain them than if you'd set a grandiose goal without considering the smaller stages. Remember the SMART objectives acronym: create goals that are precise, measurable, attainable, relevant and time-bound.

6. Take modest steps. Rather than aiming to attain a major goal all at once, divide up your primary target into several smaller

tasks. This type of to-do list—combined with time management techniques—helps you gently but gradually win the race you set for yourself. The toughest aspect of maintaining motivation is frequently the sheer length of time it takes to change a bad habit, acquire a new skill, and accomplish other objectives. By splitting up that time into tiny increments, each move forward may seem like a win of its own.

7. Talk to an adviser. If you're having a hard time remaining motivated, tap into your support network. Talk to a colleague or friend you trust. Reach out to a reliable mentor. If you feel you're dealing with your mental health, locate a trained therapist. Trained specialists can help you reprogram your brain to participate in the type of positive self-talk you need to be both joyful and driven.

Chapter 5

Setting goals and self discipline

The single most critical trait to becoming successful is self-discipline. It helps you remain focused on attaining your objectives, provides you the gumption to continue with challenging work, and enables you to overcome hurdles and pain as you push yourself to new heights.

You can't achieve your goals without discipline, so supplement your goal list with a self-discipline list; it will keep you focused on the behaviors and tasks needed to achieve what you want. For example, one of my goals is to be more visible to our customers. My discipline list includes things like "call three customers per week" and "send five thank you cards per month." Do the things on this list without fail.

Achieving your objectives might be challenging, so establish a daily "to-do" list. To remain motivated, utilize an internet application to plan your work. Checking off charges is a wonderful motivation for performing a job. And remember, your daily "to-do" list should correspond with your discipline list. That way, you won't have to be continuously searching for an excuse to avoid doing something you want to do.

With self-discipline, you'll be able to resist the need to act on urges. When you can keep yourself in control, you'll be able to remain motivated at the present and avoid toxic relationships. By adopting self-discipline, you'll be able to concentrate on the things that matter most to you, resist temptation and make choices that support your objectives.

Self-discipline is a key attribute of success. In life, you may apply self-discipline to make better choices, such as exercising, eating healthier, and spending less money on useless products. You may even be promoted if you have excellent self-discipline. A high-level self-disciplined individual may also avoid procrastination. Self-discipline also enhances your relationships and interpersonal abilities.

Self-discipline is a useful ability that may help you overcome lethargy. But it doesn't always provide you with the greatest outcomes. Forcing oneself to achieve anything will lead to success, but the results will be restricted. To strengthen self-discipline, you should concentrate on the growth of a task. This will help feed your drive to accomplish it.

When you make goals, the incentive will frequently be to move away from something unwanted and towards what you desire. Acceptance and commitment therapy is built on connecting deeply to your values and concentrating on them. It might be tough to keep motivated, but you must stay focused on your goal and trust in your ability. If you have self-discipline, you can attain your goals and be successful in life.

Chapter 6

The Importance of Setting Goal

Goals are what move us ahead in life; they are the oxygen to our dreams. They are the initial steps to any adventure we take and are also our final. Setting objectives for yourself is a technique to feed your desire.
When you make a conscious determination of reaching a given goal, even your strong subconscious is awakened and it begins inventing ideas and constructing ways to bring your passion to completion.

Why Set Goals?

1. Helps You Stay Focused: Everyone yearns to reach high heights in life, but how many

of us genuinely end up accomplishing that? Perhaps, a few.
The major reason for this is that most individuals lose attention on the road and fall.

The main value of goal setting is that it helps you stay focused to accomplish what you desire. It operates like a steering wheel that directs you along the appropriate way.
Focus is the key. You cannot afford to take your eyes off the objective even for a second. Goal planning helps you keep focused on your objectives in life.

2. Goals Help You Overcome Procrastination: When you create a goal for yourself you hold yourself accountable to accomplish the activity.
This is in full contrast with when you undertake things based on a whim and it doesn't matter whether you accomplish them or not. Goals tend to linger in your

memory and if not fulfilled they provide you a prompt reminder unconsciously.

3. Sets Obstacles: It lets you establish barriers. Setting clear, concrete objectives for yourself provides you with a hard fenceline.

It creates an invisible barrier, wherein you determine what you want, what freedoms you have, and what distractions you need to get rid of, to enhance your progress towards accomplishing your objective. It also produces some feeling of responsibility towards oneself.

4. Enables You To Manage Your Time: By defining objectives, you will be able to manage your time to your fullest advantage. You will have a clear understanding of what you have to complete in a given period.

Thus, you may devote all your energy and attention to realizing it. You may separate one large aim into several short-term goals constrained by specified constraints of time, which will make the process simpler. It enhances your productivity and efficiency tremendously.

That stated, why do individuals fail, even after making these goals?

1. Excuses!! These are generally simpler to come up with than reasons why we need to do something. They might vary from not having enough time to the stars not being precisely aligned. Whatever the case, they immobilize us.

2. Fear: Some individuals are terrified of failing or, even worse, that they may truly succeed. As such, they don't even bother attempting to reach a goal. Such individuals lack conviction in themselves and their potential.

From their perspective, if they fail, everyone would think adversely of them. And if they succeed, others will be jealous and think poorly of them. So it becomes a lose-lose scenario no matter how they look at it.

3. Not a strong enough "WHY": What does your objective mean to you? Why have you set it? When we create objectives for the wrong reasons and go after things we do not need or want; we are not compelled to pursue them, commit to them or attain them and end up losing a tremendous lot of time, energy, and money that might have been spent chasing things that resonate with us.

4. Lack of commitment to the objective: Even if individuals declare they desire to reach a given goal, in actuality, a lot of them are truly not devoted to it.

Because of this lack of commitment, individuals do not give the act of goal achievement their entire effort, and like with everything in life, if you do not give it your all, you obtain poor results. Commitment is vital for reaching any objective.

Are your everyday behaviors moving you closer to your goals? If they are not, do not expect the things in your life that you need and want altered, to change.

Chapter 7

How to Set your goals

If objectives are so vital, why do we fail to attain them? Because we don't plan the steps to get there.

A goal planning method requires you to think about the journey (in other words, how you're going to fulfill your duties) instead of simply the ultimate destination. Take a look at the steps below to get started.

1. Think about the outcomes you wish to see

Before you select a goal, take a deeper look at what you're aiming to accomplish and ask yourself the following questions:

Is this aim something you want?

Is it significant enough to devote hours of time and effort to it?

If you're not prepared to put in the time, it may not be worth pursuing.

If you develop a lengthy list of objectives to pursue all at the same time, you may have a tough time attaining any of them. Instead, utilize the questions above to establish which objectives mean the most to you right now, and then concentrate on that handful.

2. Create SMART objectives

Once you've honed in on what you genuinely want, confirm your objective fits the SMART criteria:

Specific
Measurable
Attainable
Realistic
Time-bound

The most essential component of SMART goal setting is to make your objective explicit so you can easily measure your progress and know if you fulfilled the goal. The more detailed you can be with your objective, the better the possibility you'll fulfill it.

For example, many individuals make goals to lose weight, but they don't necessarily specify how much weight they want to lose and when they want to reach this objective. A particular aim might be "I want to lose 25 pounds before the Fourth of July." This objective specifies a precise amount of weight to reduce and an end date to achieve it.

3. Write your objectives down

When you put your objectives down, they become concrete and tangible instead of a foggy notion that dwells only in your imagination. Once you've written your objectives down, keep them someplace visible––put personal goals up on your mirror or near your computer screen, post team goals up on the walls next to everyone's workstations, and include business goals in internal presentations.

This strategy encourages you to keep working on your objectives every day. As you're putting down your objectives, employ a positive tone so you remain motivated about reaching them.

4. Create an action plan

Many individuals settle on a goal but never construct an action plan to identify how precisely they will reach that objective. Your action plan should contain the overarching objective you're seeking to reach and all the actions you need to take to get there.

Don't be scared to be innovative with your action plan. Go back to your early school days, and be creative. Write down your aim using crayons, markers, or colored pencils, for example. According to Forbes, formulating an action plan in this manner

engages a different area of your brain and cements the objectives in your memory.
Use our template to develop your action plan.

5. Create a timeline
As part of your action plan, utilize a timeline builder to assist visualize responsibilities, activities, milestones, and deadlines to reach your objective. Once you've established those dates, attempt to keep to them as precisely as possible. A timeframe provides a feeling of urgency, which in turn drives you to remain on schedule and achieve your objective.

6. Take action
Now that you've planned everything out, it's time to take action. You didn't go through all that effort simply to forget about your aim. Every step that you take should lead to another until you complete your objective.

7. Re-evaluate and appraise your progress

You need to maintain your motivation high to finish your objective. Consider organizing a weekly assessment, which might entail assessing your progress and verifying your timetable. Once you realize how near the finish line is, you'll feel more driven to go through to the conclusion. If you're a bit behind schedule, make the required modifications and keep going.

Start establishing objectives

The practice of defining objectives helps you achieve quicker and more effectively. It may feed your desire and help you accomplish concrete achievements. A goal planning approach can assist you to choose how to develop objectives that are detailed, timely, and reasonable.

Create a clear path for accomplishing your development objectives with the performance development planning approach.

Chapter 8

Approach and mindset are crucial

When you are feeling stuck with your ambitions, several solutions spring to mind. Perhaps you need to study some books or explore different techniques to fulfill your objectives. But another path to investigate is to improve your goal-setting mentality.

Like with everything in the self-improvement realm and beyond, attitude counts. How you interpret your challenges and your general belief and thinking process may govern many things. Some are more direct while others we won't see until down the road.

With this in mind, here are some things you might consider while you are creating or cultivating a goal-setting attitude.

Why Does Mindset Matter?

Knowing your attitude is one thing, but it's another to realize why it's worth the effort. Why is it worth putting your time and effort into it?

The greatest reason is what was discussed above: your entire route is defined by your thinking, which is impacted by how you view the world. It is your general perspective that is going to influence your success or failure, how you handle adversities, and more. [1]

It's not to suggest all you need is an attitude to attain success, but your mindset will affect every element of your life and will steer you ahead.

If your thinking suggests that your work is bad or that you won't go very far, you'll behave accordingly. You won't be working as hard or have little energy since you spend so much time thinking about the fact your job is tedious or unfulfilling.

On the flip, if you feel your job is meaningful, stimulating, and rewarding, you'll wake up with possibly more energy and be generally delighted to accomplish work. There is always going to be some action – or inactivity – dependent on your mentality.

How this applies to a goal-setting mentality is that how you establish, work, and attain those objectives is dependent on your vision of the world. The activities and the particular specifics of those acts are all controlled by your understanding of your aims.

It's why some individuals who accomplish a large objective feel trapped once they achieve it. Some individuals were exclusively focused on one objective and didn't diversify or have other things to aim for.

All the same, some individuals will struggle because somewhere along the road, how you perceive yourself, your method, your objective, or any other part may not be optimal for you.

How Can I Develop A Goal-Setting Mindset? As noted earlier, chances are probable that a portion of your goal-setting attitude is incorrect or it's not serving you effectively. It's utilized as a mental hurdle, and you make reasons to either ignore it and attempt to go on or feel stuck. You want to accomplish it but end up becoming irritated or coming up with some reason to not do it.

Like with other things, this is something that you can correct, and part of it is to grow your attitude further or differently. The sequence of activities you may conduct for this are various thus there's no better way. Select one – or more – from the choices below and discover what they can achieve for you.

1. Rethink Your Purpose

This may be divided into two sections: the objective itself and the motive to pursue this goal.

It's these two distinct characteristics that form your aim and may determine your total mindset.

Are you establishing this goal because it makes you feel good? Or are you making this goal because you want or need to attain this?

Once you select objectives that matter a lot to you and that you want to strive towards, you'll be able to recognize the difference between these two characteristics better. But the most apparent distinction between feel-good objectives and genuine goals is the motivation to fulfill them.

This is when the second part gets in — your rationale, you are why for the beginning. You'll discover feel-good objectives don't have a compelling purpose. It's something that you can procrastinate and you don't contemplate the implications. It's something you can do later.

2. Don't Try, Make It Happen

Even the way you express things in your brain or your voice might affect your behavior as well. Many individuals would state in their resolutions that they will "try" to accomplish anything. They never use "I will." What happens after that is predictable. Three months later, they're nowhere near their target.

The difficulty in this scenario is the amount of dedication one has to their objectives in the first place. Like the last point, if you're lacking commitment, you're not going to dig deep for a personal purpose to accomplish anything. You'll say things but not mean any of it.

My suggestion is to shift your mindset so that you are more focused on making things happen. If you are committed to something, take the action and trust that you'll get somewhere with this.

3. Look for Progression in Many Places

Naturally, advancement towards a goal is excellent, and individuals want to see themselves pushing the needle. But monitoring progress all the time might be negative as well.

What if you're not improving as rapidly as you desire or your expectations are too high for the results you received?

These factors might lead individuals to lose motivation or feel like they're spending time going nowhere and quit up. It's at this period when I propose that you search for growth in other areas.

For example, individuals might sometimes feel depressed when their objective is to lose weight and see that the weight scale isn't shifting much or at all despite their efforts. While most individuals quit up or become frustrated, try looking at other aspects of your life. Do you find certain moves to be easier? Have you made any lifestyle changes? Are particular jobs easier to do? The idea is that by exercising, you may not be losing weight right now, but you are growing your muscles more and making them better than before.

Another way to look at this is to remind yourself that you are making more progress than someone who is still thinking about doing something rather than doing it - even if it doesn't feel like it.

4. Upgrade Yourself

Sometimes you establish lofty objectives - goals that are difficult to fulfill now at this moment. That's alright. The key to creating greater objectives is to recognize that certain goals need a particular degree of excellence from you.

Recognize that to reach certain objectives, sometimes you need to enhance your talents in particular areas or gain new skills entirely. Whatever the situation is, look at the numerous components required to accomplish what you desire. Don't be scared to conduct some research and check what other people are talking about on the issue.

5. Tell Yourself It's Okay to Fail

Another crucial part of a goal-setting attitude is to recognize that failing is alright. As much as you want to attain a goal in one attempt, odds are you won't. You're going to fail or stall out or whatever.

The idea is to not consider these situations as anything truly horrible. They're setbacks, yes, but it's not the end of the road. All that's required from you at this stage is to make some adjustments to your present structure - how you are planning objectives, establishing goals, and taking action on them.

Remind yourself that failure is a chance for you to make things better than they were before. It's a time to regroup and make things better for you and that much simpler to attain your objectives in the future. The only true negative is that failure might be a heavy blow to you at first.

6 . Believe in Yourself

The final advice to establish a better goal-setting mentality is to believe in yourself. As clichéd as it seems, there is weight put on your belief in oneself. It all boils down to your thinking.

If you don't believe in yourself, you're not going to be as devoted to anything. You could even look at your failures as grounds to never do anything like that again since it ended owing to your claimed lack of expertise.

It's easy to think that way and led to a downward cycle of negativity, but deep down, you know that negativity isn't real. All that you have to do is find a way to believe in yourself more and to keep working at it.

It's remarkable what pure tenacity and adaptation can do for you in completing a goal. And it all begins with believing in yourself

Chapter 9

The Value of Rewarding Yourself

It's crucial to reward yourself, and your team, as soon as you achieve a critical job or target. Why? By rewarding yourself in the present, your brain produces favorable feelings, leading to the knowledge that your efforts result in a positive reward. By doing this regularly, your brain will learn to attach pleasure to finishing the activity or target and gravitate towards it in the future.

So what incentives work best?

Common incentives typically include:

A pause to watch a beloved program towards the conclusion of a study session

A day off after a week of hard work Or a short vacation away at the end of a successful trimester.

To be successful, incentives should be something fun for you — a session at the gym may be a wonderful reward for a fitness fanatic, but can be punishment for anyone else!"

One thing to bear in mind is the contrast between internal and outward rewards. External rewards are objects or experiences that you may treat yourself to - such as a day off, a great lunch, or a getaway. On the other hand, internal rewards relate to something inside you — your feelings and states of mind. Internal incentives for the study could include emotions of pleasure after accomplishing a challenging job, happiness at being a step closer to your objectives, or just the delight of being engrossed in a work.

Interestingly, studies have shown that in the long term, internal incentives are more successful at motivating pupils; you are more likely to study hard if you feel good about it. Therefore, take the time to allow yourself to experience the wonderful sensations connected with learning.

Don't forget!
It’s vital to not mix treating yourself with procrastinating. Rewarding oneself is when you have finished a goal, rather than inhibiting yourself from accomplishing anything.

www.ingramcontent.com/pod-product-compliance
Lightning Source LLC
LaVergne TN
LVHW020606160826
845677LV00020B/3802

* 9 7 9 8 8 4 8 2 2 7 4 6 8 *